I0824932

Team BLOOM's

WREATHS

150 IDEAS FOR EVERY SEASON

Laura Marx

Wildflower.Media

PREFACE

Wreaths are an absolute classic design style, and they welcome visitors at the front door. But they also spray the magic of the respective season on the wall and immediately cast a spell on the viewer. No wonder, because what more beautiful, natural floral art could there be than wreaths? Wreaths can be designed in a variety of ways and are often very long-lasting, depending on the choice of materials. With the numerous possibilities that open up for each season, I would prefer to create a new wreath and hang it up every week. Whether in autumn, with colorful leaves, chestnuts and rose hips; in winter with festive fir, cones and Christmas balls; in spring, with delicate bulb flowers, Easter eggs and feathers; or in summer, with colorful flowers, grasses and ribbons, this book offers lots of new and modern design ideas for wreaths. Would you like to get started right away? Then flip through the following chapters, and let yourself be inspired! The techniques for the various wreaths are marked with icons and explained in detail in the Techniques section. So, even beginners get their money's worth. I hope you enjoy recreating these designs for yourself!

Laura Marx

KNOW HOW!
The icons below indicate which techniques the individual wreaths are based on. These are explained in detail in the Techniques section.
Threading
Drilling and Wiring
Pinning
Adhering
Picking
Wrapping
Winding

FOREWORD 2 - 3

AUTUMN 6 - 35

WINTER 36 - 65

SPRING 66 - 83

SUMMER 84 - 99

TECHNIQUES 100 - 117

CREDITS 120

AUTUMN

The third season, with its abundance of lush flowers and bright fruits, is particularly suitable for natural door and wall designs. Whether rose hips, chestnuts, lantern flowers, ornamental apples, colorful foliage, ivy, hops, dahlias, mature hydrangeas or heather — the selection seems limitless and offers plenty of options for very different colors and styles. Fabric as well as dry fruits, grasses, leaves or flowers can also be used for permanent wreaths. Draw on the fullness of the season!

TIP

For wreaths with a rural patchwork look, simply combine knitwear, fabric, flowers, grasses and the like, and mix it up carefree!

PATCHWORK

Flower quilt in the shape of a wreath: This wreath is wrapped with various knitted remnants and strips of fabric. It shines in warm autumnal hues. Pins hold the pieces together. In between, dry florals, such as everlasting flowers, yarrow, sorrel, tansies, grasses and grains, are either plugged in or glued on. As a final touch, wrap some burdock around the arrangement.

  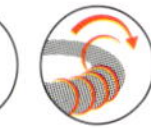

COLORFUL INSIGHTS

For this patchwork work of art, a wreath form is wrapped with colorful scraps of fabric, then covered with an embroidered blanket affixed with hot-glue. The underneath fabric can be pulled out through incisions with a sharp knife. Everlasting flowers are glued on or attached with pins and give off a wildflower charm.

Pink binding wire not only holds the bundles of straw together but also adds colorful accents.

CLEVERLY BUNDLED

With the help of wire, fabric scraps formed into tuffs, as well as grasses, everlasting flowers and drumsticks that are bundled together, create abundance. Wire also helps here. The bundles can then be picked into or glued onto the straw wreath base.

WOOLLY FRAME

For a wall decoration with a cozy factor, fix several layers of wool and fabric remnants with adhesive and hot-glue on the inside and outside of a straw wreath base. Insert bundles of grasses firmly in the middle, and place dry everlasting flowers in between, securing them with pins or hot-glue.

Silver wire, pearls, fine ribbons and the like act as decorative elements.

PETITE ROUNDS

This is how guests can be welcomed with an impression. The thin wreath is based on a wire ring covered with olive leaves, attached with a visible wrapping of shiny silver wire. Beads are threaded onto smaller wire rings; leaves, moss or ribbon are wrapped; and silk flowers are glued to the larger rings. To finish, tie together with ribbons at the top of the large wreath.

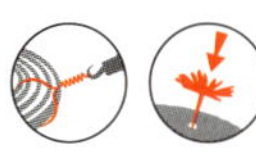

RUSTIC BARK

The contrast between the rough birch bark and the delicate permanent flowers is what makes this door wreath so attractive. For this design, a ready-made birch wreath is wired to a dry-floral-foam wreath form. Its edge is then decorated with the flowers and leaves. A knotted ribbon tail completes the weatherproof piece of jewelry.

Birch bark and permanent flowers create an exciting contrast.

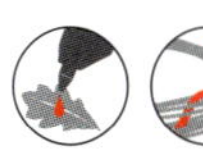

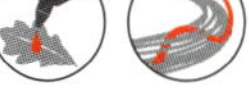

CASUALLY TWISTED

A permanent door ornament can also be made from flexible dogwood branches that are wound into a decorative wreath. Alternatively, a ready-made base can also be purchased. Permanent dahlia blooms and dried grass are attached to it with hot-glue.

TIP

A wreath can be easily made from wire, which can be shaped as desired.

GREEN DROP

Instead of being round, this extravagant hanging wreath is presented in an attractive teardrop shape. For this design, unwound wire is formed into a mesh structure, into which boxwood, ornamental apples, berries and the like can easily be inserted. In addition, colored bast is woven crisscross through it and then wrapped around the two wire ends.

FRUITY FOLIAGE

With bright fruits and leaves, the full abundance of the third season comes into your own four walls. The sides of a straw wreath are covered with maple leaves using liquid floral adhesive/cold glue. Wire ornamental apples, double rose hips, lantern flowers and peacock hats, and arrange them onto the front. In addition, everything can be sealed with spray adhesive. Then wind clematis around the inner and outer edges of the wreath.

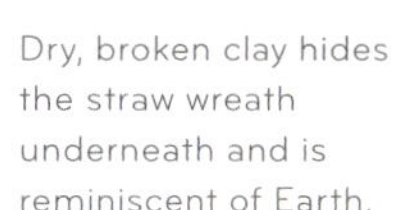

Dry, broken clay hides the straw wreath underneath and is reminiscent of Earth.

TONE ON TONE

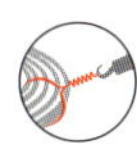  

Clay, mixed with a little water and wood glue, transforms a simple straw wreath base into an original frame for the florals glued into a large ball of wire in the center.

FOREST WALK

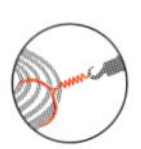 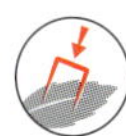  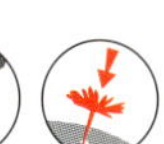

The materials for this eye-catcher come from a foray through autumnal nature and are pinned, picked or glued to a moss-covered straw wreath base.

Concentric rings of individual botanical materials form a lush wreath.

CLEVERLY COMBINED

For this door wreath, which widens toward the bottom, the grain heads and the tendrils (bines) of the hops serve as design elements. The goldenrod and the fruits of St. John's wort are wired onto rings of corrugated mesh wire. The wreath is finished at the top with a wrap of binding wire.

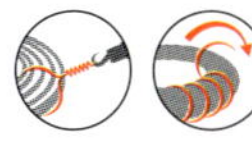

PLAYFUL ORBS

A cheerful accent is created by cutting a straw wreath in half at one point, spreading it apart and pinning a wad of coiled winding wire in the gap. Pick or glue rose hips and felt balls into the wire section. Wrap the rest of the wreath with boxwood, making it wider toward the bottom.

Felt balls in various colors and sizes add a playful touch.

FRESH BLOOMING JOY

For the transition from late summer to autumn, this fresh wreath of flowers adorns the door for a short time. Dahlias, lavender, lantern flowers, hydrangeas, montbretia, artificial plants, dill, lady's mantle, various fruits, buds and leaves are worked into a wet-floral-foam ring that has a plastic or rigid foam base. Affix long ribbons at the bottom.

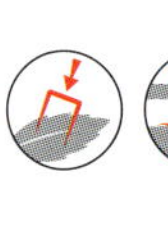 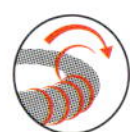

LUMINOSITY

Not only do lantern flowers, berries and safflowers shine within this autumnal gem, the former are placed onto a string of lights, which creates a sophisticated effect. The straw wreath base is first covered with Roman wrapping tape (wreath gusset tape), and then covered with moss, ivy, lichen, twigs and the like. Then, the string of lights is simply wrapped around the wreath form.

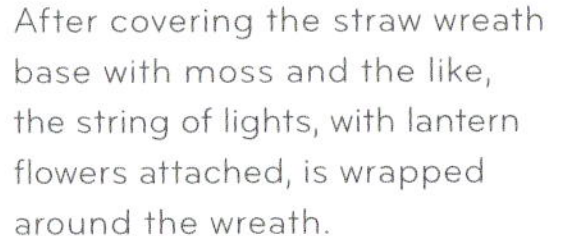

After covering the straw wreath base with moss and the like, the string of lights, with lantern flowers attached, is wrapped around the wreath.

SPLASH OF COLOR

Instead of all colors, lantern flowers shine only in orange. The LED light string to which they are attached can be concealed with moss, lichen, alpine rose and rose hip branches, pieces of bark and acorns, which are pinned, picked or glued to the straw wreath base. Everything comes into its own in front of the rustic wooden wall.

The lantern flowers are placed onto the bulbs of a string of battery-operated lights and affixed with wire.

SMALL LANTERNS

In this arrangement, too, lantern flowers placed onto lights play the main role. But red mountain ash berries and blue-black ivy berries also add autumn charm and are held in place with pins or wire. The base of the wreath is covered with moss and various types of lichen. There are also blueberry and alpine rose branches as well as barberry.

RIBBON TAIL

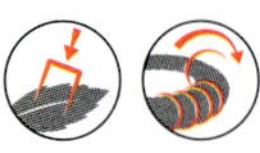

Lichen and lantern flowers are the main focus of this wreath. The straw wreath from is first covered with felt and decorated long hanging ribbons.

PERMANENTLY BEAUTIFUL

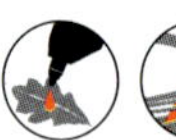

A twig wreath serves as the base of this design. Star scabiosas, empty acorn cups and the like are attached to it with hot glue.

Affix the lantern flowers onto the lights with wire.

ALPINE CHARM

Deer antlers worked into a lush green wreath create the magic of a cabin even on the living-room wall at home. The light string, with green lantern flowers, is wrapped around the straw wreath base and then surrounded by ivy, conifer branches, lichen, swamp-oak leaves, pieces of bark and star scabiosas. Simply attach them with pins, picks or glue. There are also long ribbons.

MAGNIFICENT HEATHER

Such a voluminous heather wreath, in colors from pink to fresh green, looks great, even without any additional botanical materials! To make it look so lush, the stems of heather are wired closely together. You will be delighted by them throughout the entire autumn season.

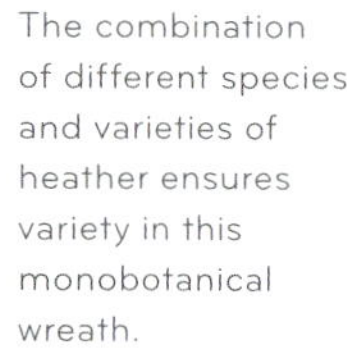

The combination of different species and varieties of heather ensures variety in this monobotanical wreath.

CONEFLOWER HEADS 

The eye-catching flower heads of coneflower blooms are threaded onto aluminum wire together with the small cut stems. Fasten a bow of grass at the top with vine binding wire.

HOP SEASON  

Hop tendrils (bines) can be wound into a dense wreath, or individual pieces can be wrapped around a straw wreath. If you want to save time, buy a ready-made specimen!

TIP

The robust buds of common heather retain their color even when dry and do not drop.

LONG-LASTING BUDS

The artistic infructescence of ivy and summer linden, fluffy clematis, thyme and green leaves, which are wrapped around the straw mat, can also be combined with colorful heather. This creates permanent jewelry for the wall. Long strips of fabric serve as a suspension and repeat the flower colors.

COUNTRY HOUSE CHIC

Green heather, wild carrot and meadow grasses make a particularly casual autumn wreath when they are loosely wrapped with wire around a wire wreath ring—long tendrils of lantern flowers, driftwood tied to a coarse cord, and blackberries.

ROSY CENTER

For the filigree flower ring, a handmade wire wreath ring is covered with heather, sea lavender and hydrangea florets. Yarrow and star umbels are wrapped around. Deliberately create the wreath to be narrower at one end. Finally, hang a water-filled wine glass with a white rose blossom on a natural cord.

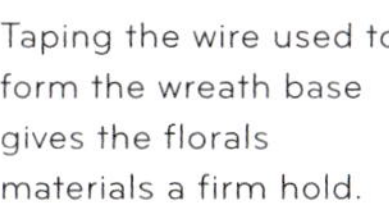

Taping the wire used to form the wreath base gives the florals materials a firm hold.

TIP

If you use a wet-floral-foam wreath form for a hanging wreath, wrap it in foil or plastic wrap so that it does not drip.

FORMALITY

This teardrop-shaped wreath base is formed with wire mesh (chicken wire) and contains wet floral foam wrapped with foil or plastic wrap. Tie bundles of heather onto the form with twine. Insert flower stems into the floral foam and the plums on toothpicks.

HIGHLIGHTS

In the middle of the heather, colorful lantern flowers flash, which are put onto a string of miniature lights. The straw wreath base is first wrapped with the light strand and then with felt wool.

PURE NATURE

With this rustic door decoration, a willow wreath serves as a base for various branches, which are drilled and then connected with toothpicks or wood picks. For better stability, some places can also be fixed with glue and/or wire. Long grasses act as a green element, which are interwoven and fixed at the ends with a cord. Pull this through the center of the wreath, and tie it at the top.

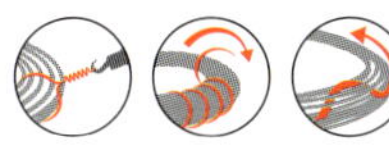

GREEN TENDRILS

A willow wreath forms the base of this design. It is first wrapped with grass that is attached with decorative wire. Then defoliate the rose and blackberry tendrils, and wind them around the willow form (make sure to wear gloves). Possibly also affix with wire. A special eye-catcher is also created by another wrapping of grass. Use nylon thread for invisible suspension.

One part of the wreath is attractively accentuated with a wrapping of grass.

WRAPPED WILDLY

The casual meadow wreath is very easy to make. Simply wrap a straw wreath with white stretch film and then loosely with grass, leaving a few white spaces in between. Cover some areas with a white gauze bandage to catch the eyes. Large zinc nails fix and act as an optical element.

TIP

You can also do without flowers: The mix of red and white berries ensures liveliness.

FILIGREE DANCE

At the door, a nice welcome for visitors! The dry stems of rapeseed can be twisted into a filigree wreath. Fix with wire. Then simply pull through the snowberry branches with their white fruits. The red mountain-ash berries are bundled with wire and attached to the frame.

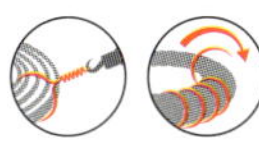

APPLE FESTIVAL

Thanksgiving in a completely different way: In this wreath, the sophisticated look of which consists of the coiled vines of wild clematis, apples tempt you to nibble. The branch is attached with wire. A base made of floral foam or straw is suitable as a base.

Sea buckthorn is not only a treat for the eyes but the berries also exude a wonderfully sweet scent.

FRAGRANT DECORATION

To make the wreath look particularly tight, first wrap the straw wreath base with orange tape so that no straw shows through. Then cut sea-buckthorn branches into small pieces, and attach them to the wreath base. Bare branches flash out cheekily here and there.

RED PEARLS

Enthusiastic autumn decorations to hang up: The double wreath is made with two different-sized rings, so the hoops swing back and forth freely. The branches are simply wrapped around each wire ring with twine or binding wire before connecting the rings.

The color mix makes the wreath look particularly three-dimensional.

COLOR FIREWORKS

The luminous fruit clusters of lantern flowers set the tone in this wreath design. They are worked into a wet, foil-covered floral-foam wreath form, along with star scabiosas, arable herb, burdock and stonecrop. Place the tendrils of the lantern flowers on top, and fasten with pins or picks.

Decorative wires wound around the wire wreath form are reminiscent of lantern-flower stems.

STYLISH

Unusual: Shape a length of thick wire into a ring, and wrap decorative wires, in different colors, closely together. Glue lantern flowers and burdock fruit onto their ends.

LUSH SPLENDOR

The whole cornucopia of the colorful season can be found in this wet-floral-foam wreath: dahlias, coneflowers, coreopsis, strawflowers, lantern flowers, helenium, tansies, sea buckthorn, rose hips, clematis and apples on wood sticks are simply tucked away. Foil wrapped around the wreath prevents it from dripping. Finally, silver poplar leaves are glued on, as desired.

Work in autumn colors alternately from green to yellow and orange to red.

OFF THE BRANCH

The wreath here is effectively framed by a crooked branch and attached stones. Form the base with tendrils and rattan. Pine cones, some of which are wrapped with cord, garden foxtail and field horsetail are pinned or glued in. Tightly knotted hemp cord attaches the wreath and stones to the branch.

FOR NUTCRACKERS

The little rusty squirrel sits on the wreath like in a rustic nest. Like the nuts and cones, it is fixed with hot-glue. First cover a straw wreath with moss, then with pine branches and dry clematis, which are loosely placed around the base. Thick jute cord serves as a suspension.

Chestnuts have a long shelf life and are great highlights.

RUSTIC JEWELS

Natural jewelry for the wall or door: Chestnut after chestnut line up like shiny pearls, which are inserted into a straw wreath base with toothpicks. Fill in the gaps with clematis, which, in turn, is held in place with decorative wire. A rustic branch, which is attached above with wire and fixed at various points with hot glue, adds the finishing touch.

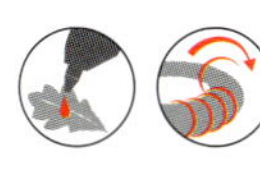

ABUNDANCE OF FLOWERS

The lush, fresh green hydrangea blossoms, which are wrapped around the wreath with wire, dry out over time. They lose volume in the process, but they are still pretty to look at. Individual ginkgo leaves that match the color of the flowers are applied with liquid floral adhesive/cold glue.

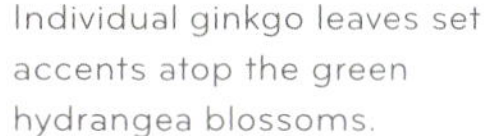

Individual ginkgo leaves set accents atop the green hydrangea blossoms.

COLORFUL FOLIAGE

Many different brightly colored leaves are attached to the straw wreath base in several layers with spray adhesive. Simply fan them out to create more volume. Ornamental apples, placed on toothpicks, form a lively eye-catcher in between.

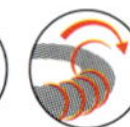

RIBBON JEWELRY

For a fashionable stripe look, a straw wreath base is first wrapped with a wide dark red satin ribbon and then with a narrow, lighter satin ribbon, which are fixed in place with pins. At the top, the wreath is adorned with a shiny bow, which is formed from organza ribbon. Tufts of pine are knotted on long hanging ribbons.

ON THE WIRE

With the barbed-wire plant cut into small pieces, this wreath takeson an airy look. Glued-on star scabiosas form a subtle dance.

RED BERRIES

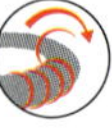

Rose hips in various sizes, wrapped with wire, and a strip of upturned ornamental apples on toothpicks make this bright wreath so attractive.

Nice detail: The blue-black berries of the wild vine sit on reddish branches.

PLAY OF COLORS

In autumn, hydrangea blooms change color in the most beautiful shades and create dreamy effects on the wall. They are attached to a straw wreath base with winding wire. Dark berries, which are simply wired in, provide a little loosening up in between.

WINTER

Snow flurries, sparkling lights and festive sparkle—the cold season has a special magic inherent in it, which can also be used in the design of wreaths. Coniferous evergreens, mosses or boxwood are good for bases. Cones, nuts and fruits, as well as Christmas accessories such as balls, stars, cinnamon sticks and even cookies, can be combined. Fairy lights or artificial snow create original effects. Fabrics, ribbon, wool and felt make them really cozy.

Simple cardboard stars can be nicely pepped up with a wrap of two-tone cord.

DECORATED BRANCHES

This wreath is a feast for the eyes. A straw wreath is partially wrapped with wool and sisal ribbon in cheerful colors. The red-dogwood branches are attached to wreath with wire pins, as are the holly and mistletoe branches, as well as all kinds of accessories such as stars, balls and ornamental apples.

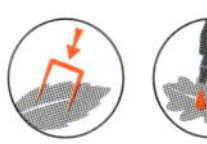

HOUSE TO HOUSE

Corrugated cardboard, adorned with various ribbons and paper, is glued inside and outside around the straw wreath and as a cuff at the front. Circular pieces also serve as Christmas balls. The center is filled with moss, juniper, larch cones, holly berries, ornamental apples, bare branches and wood stars. Most items are pinned, picked or wire on and, if necessary, also glued.

The corrugated cardboard is decorated with ribbons and paper, all of which are attached with spray adhesive.

FESTIVE PACKAGE

The centerpiece of this festive wall decoration is a straw wreath wrapped with ribbons and dishcloths. Wire rings and rattan cane are placed around this and affixed with wire. The former are either wrapped in juniper, boxwood or wool, or ornamental apples are threaded onto them. Finally, fabric stars are attached with hot-glue, and gift boxes are wired on.

 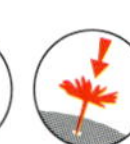 

CHILDLIKE CHARM

Boxwood is attached to the outside of a straw wreath and, thus, forms a green frame for candied and sugared fruits, matte red glass balls, apple slices, aniseed stars, nuts, cones, stars and felt ribbon. These are either picked in or glued on.

JINGLING ACCESSORIES

With a wrap of red wool and long ribbons to which childlike accessories are knotted, a green wreath quickly becomes a festive eye-catcher.

LOVELY DOUBLE

  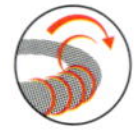

This playful wreath is wrapped with pastel-colored wool, centered with a ring of false cypress and then decorated with pins, stars and cake lace, using hot-glue.

From the Christmas bakery: Cookies and gingerbread give off a sweet scent and have a long shelf life.

SWEET SEDUCTION

A cardboard ring, slightly smaller than the underlying straw wreath wrapped with false cypress, is wrapped with wool yarn in various colors. Ribbons and yarn can be used to tie on delicious cookies and gingerbread, as well as colorful stars and cones. Now fix the resulting festive ring atop the green wreath with liquid floral adhesive/cold glue.

TIP

Arrange blades of whitewashed grass in loops, to reinforce the spherical style.

SNOWBALL FIGHT

The matte white balls are reminiscent of snowballs. Mulberry bark and dry whitewashed grass also give this casual wreath a natural look. The flowers and accessories are wired and/or hot-glued to a straw wreath. Finally, tie multiple floor-length lengths of ribbon at the top.

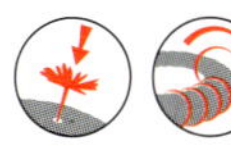

JUST GREAT

A magical wall decoration that is always a pretty sight: Torn strips of fabric and wool are knotted around the straw wreath, and crocheted lace is affixed with pins. Pin a small wreath of false cypress to the inner perimeter.

The knots remain intentionally visible and act as a decorative element.

PLAYFUL HODGEPODGE

The mix of cones, dried apple slices, various decorative stars and mushrooms, cinnamon sticks, felt wool, ribbons and lace is sure to put everyone in a good mood. The accessories are held by wire or hot-glue on the moss-covered straw wreath base.

The pine cones are attached to the wreath with wire.

ALPINE HAPPINESS

Bring the alpine aesthetic straight to your home! Winding tendrils of wild wine serve as a base for this wall decoration, which is wrapped with ivy, silky pine and arborvitae branches. Cones are attached to it with wire, and the balls, nuts and stars are hot-glued. Red-and-white checked ribbons exude rural charm.

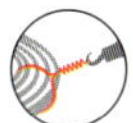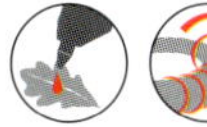

WOODEN HIGHLIGHT

The highlight of the straw wreath form wrapped in juniper branches is the wood-disc structure glued into the center. It is also entwined with tendrils of wild wine, which are attached with picks or pins. Dry twigs and tufts of pine, as well as cones and stars, complete the arrangement and are attached with paper-covered bind wire or hot-glue.

A wood-disc piece can be bought in stores or made yourself with hot-glue.

MADE QUICKLY

A smaller vine wreath, a rustic cowbell, a star and coniferous branches are tied with red-and-white fabric ribbons atop a finished pine wreath.

CLASSIC POINSETTIA

On the rustic wreath of conifers, a poinsettia flower in a water tube provides a great accent. Pundulous ribbons and felt stars repeat the color.

Ribbons and green wrapped rings surround the waxed cone ring.

NATURAL CONTRASTS

The densely joined tenon scales, which form the basis of this door decoration, appear downright frosty due to a coating of wax. This creates a nice contrast to the wrapped rings made of moss, olive branches, eucalyptus, thyme and juniper, which are attached to the cones with picks or pins. Let the ribbons hang down long.

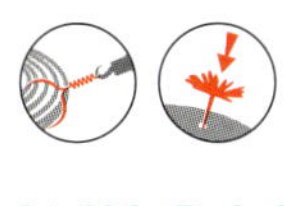

WILDLIFE

For this door wreath, a dry-floral-foam wreath form is decorated with coniferous evergreens before a ball garland, cones and stars are added. Wire helps with this. Antlers add an attractive forest attribute. Ribbons serve as suspension as well as jewelry.

Conifer branches and the like can be simply inserted into the dry-floral-foam wreath form.

CHRISTMAS STAR

The wrapped wreath beautifully stages stars made of cardboard wrapped with fabric and cones. A metal ring is the base used for the evergreen wreath.

ROUND TRIO

Three-fold beautiful: The red rose-hip wreath and the green coniferous wreath, as well as ribbons and decorative stars, are attached to a whitewashed vine wreath with hot-glue.

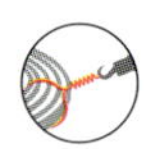 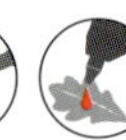 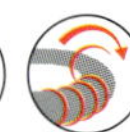

CABIN MAGIC

A naturally wild wreath has found its place above the mantelpiece, between hunting trophies. Nostalgic suspenders, leather stars finished with copper leaf and pine branches banded with wire adorn the straw wreath base, which is wrapped in fresh juniper and decorative wire. Decorative items are attached with wire or hot-glue.

GOOD HUNTING

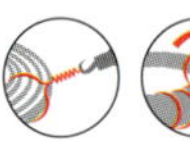 

The deer head with patina turns a pine wreath into unique winter jewelry. It is attached to the base with binding wire.

ORNATE BRANCH

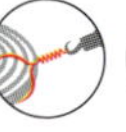 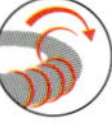

Variation: Instead of the metal deer, the focus is now on the attached branch, which is wrapped with colorful yarns and fabrics and decorated with acorns, balls and stars.

Attached straw stars and tufts of pine give a natural look.

HANGING GAME

Quickly done: Cover a straw wreath with moss, securing it with decorative wire. Hang on coconut coir fiber rope, then hang straw stars, tree decorations, pine tufts and colored peppers on various ribbons and cords that are suspended below the wreath.

WINDOW DECORATIONS

In front of a candlelit window, this simple wreath of fresh holly comes into its own. For this design, bundles of twigs are bound onto a straw wreath base. Magnificent moiré ribbons are loosely knotted around the top and bottom sections of the wreath.

With the help of a wire ring, the fruit-covered branches remain in a round wreath shape.

BRIGHT RED

This wreath is adorned with with fruity red holly berries. The decorative branches are affixed onto a wire ring with winding wire. A color-matching bow gives a festive, elegant flair. An eye-catcher both inside and outside!

Various blue ribbons tied at the top pick up the color of the berries.

TWO IN ONE

A fine wreath of blue viburnum and red skimmia berries is wrapped with wire in no time at all. It is decorated with small larch cones and a blue ribbon anchoring tufts of pine. The cones are attached with hot-glue. The piece of jewelry unfolds its full effect on a wreath base of whitewashed branches. The two specimens are connected with wire.

TIP

A neutral wreath can be given a festive note quickly with decorative accessories such as self-designed Styrofoam stars.

GREAT STARS

With wall paint, wood picks and rubber bands, glued-on Styrofoam stars become interesting eye-catchers on the wreath made of spruce, thyme and rose hips. A moss-wrapped straw wreath hides beneath the botanical and decorative materials. Christmas ribbons, which are attached with wire, form additional accents.

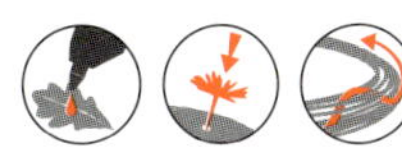

FLORAL WHEEL

The unusual wheel made of twisted and interlocked hardwood and pine branches is reminiscent of ornate ice crystals on the windows. Green and red apples are wired onto the branches, and whitewashed cones, stars and hearts are glued on.

All kinds of accessories are incorporated into the stable framework made of branches.

O CHRISTMAS TREE

The radiant center of the lush spruce-wrapped straw wreath form is a decorative white ceramic fir tree, which sits enthroned atop a hodgepodge of small colorful Christmas ornaments. The ornaments are affixed onto the straw wreath base with hot-glue.

NATURAL SPLENDOR

In the sweeping wreath, pine needles bundled with white wool and small stars contrast discreetly with the brown of the cones and pieces of root. The latter are attached to a straw wreath base wrapped in gray wool secured with decorative wire. Glue moss into open spaces, and glue bunches of pine, whitewashed cones and stars on top.

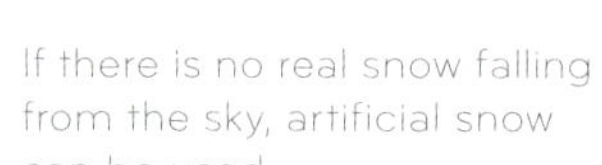

If there is no real snow falling from the sky, artificial snow can be used.

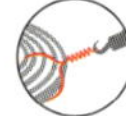 

WINTER DREAM

The rustic outdoor wreath made of conifer branches wound on a straw wreath base gets its special charm from the bare branches. Also shaped into a wreath, they are attached to the base of conifer with wire. Hanging on checkered fabric ribbon, the decorative piece greets visitors outdoors.

Stars covered with sugar or glitter convey a frosty, wintry impression.

FROSTY SHINE

Whether on a stone wall or a front door, this winter gem will always be well received. Lichen branches, giant goldenrod, larch cones, silver poplar leaves, birch bark and various decorative stars are pulled through the vine wreath or attached with hot-glue. The pine needles are adhered with spray adhesive.

FOR THE BIRDS

The wreath of mistletoe is not only a popular winter landing spot for glass bird ornaments but also a graceful window decoration. The twigs are wrapped onto a metal ring, and a bare branch is attached to it with wire. The birdies can simply be clamped on, and the stars are attached with hot-glue.

MAGIC MISTLETOE

Mistletoe and grevillea leaves are loosely wrapped around a straw wreath. White lace and fabric ribbons provide romance, and ice crystals and artificial snow add wintry flair. Cones and balls, dipped in light green paint, are tied to the ribbons.

BRIGHT WHITE

  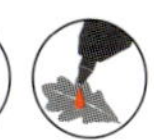 

Around a straw wreath, which is topped with a wreath of whitewashed thorny milkweed, is a ring of mussel cypress. Glue in the cones and leaves.

FLUFFY WRAPPING

Juniper and clematis form the wrapping for this wreath. Grevillea leaves are simply pushed under the wire securing the greenery to the straw wreath base, and ribbons and tags are attached at the top.

WINTER FRESHNESS

The modern wreath of coniferous evergreens is presented in fresh green and brilliant white. Apples, glittering stars, whitewashed cones and twigs, leaves, and dark berries catch the eyes, and they are secured into the wreath with toothpicks, wire and/or hot-glue.

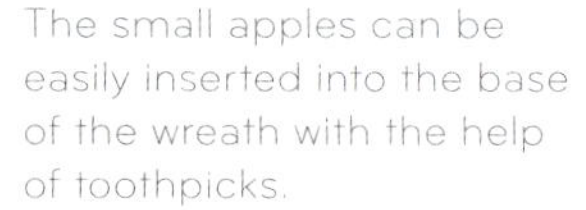

The small apples can be easily inserted into the base of the wreath with the help of toothpicks.

FLORAL SCARF

Pretty and fashionable: A straw wreath wrapped with false cypress stands out with a decorative floral scarf. To do this, wires in silver and ice blue are woven and pinned on top of the wreath. Silver leaf, bleached euphoria, cones, glitter stars, mirror berries and cord are worked into the scarf.

GOLDEN SHINE

A straw wreath, wrapped in different colored wool threads, is given a natural touch by branches of fresh black pine and mistletoe that are wired through the center. The pine branches are banded with gold aluminum wire, and Christmas ornaments are suspended from them and underline the elegant color scheme.

WAXED CHIC

Eye-catcher: The ring of waxed cones is framed by a narrower ring of olive branches, silver leaves, juniper and fir. Fix a shimmering bow at the top, with ribbons and ball-shaped ornaments hanging from it.

The white wax coating gives the cones a refined look

GAME OF FORMS

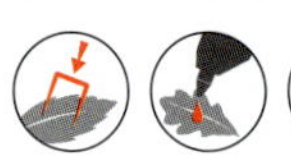

Here, a cone wreath is glued atop a dry-floral-foam wreath form, the edges of which are covered with wool and pieces of branches. Adhere a small juniper wreath to the inside.

NOBLE CONES

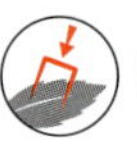

Another variant: A cone wreath is affixed with picks or pins onto a Styrofoam wreath form encircled with florals. Glue Christmas balls and cones into the gaps.

TIP

Real flowers stay fresh for a long time in water tubes and can be easily exchanged.

DELICATE FLOWERS

Dried twigs are attached to an iron ring using the drill technique. Wire water tubes onto the twigs with paper-covered binding wire, and fill with flowers. Mahonia berries, juniper, olive and eucalyptus branches are pulled through the wreath. Cones, stars and balls are adhered with tape or hot-glue.

RUSTIC VINES

A simple vine wreath is playfully embellished with colorful accessories. About a third of the wreath is wrapped with various ribbons and cord, and a piece of bark is glued to it. Coniferous evergreen and twisted dogwood wreaths, as well as rolled wood shavings, cones and hearts, are suspended on long ribbons.

NUTTY MIX

Peanuts, hazelnuts and almonds; pine; star anise; and glass balls combine to form a decorative mixture. They are hot-glued onto a dry-floral-foam wreath form wrapped in felt. Silver ornaments, hanging on magnificent cords, attract attention.

Materials can be easily attached to dry foam.

WILLKOMMEN

Fluffy! A dry-floral-foam wreath form, covered with magic floss, is the ideal base for walnut shell halves and small glass ornaments, which are affixed with hot-glue. Tree-of-life twigs wrapped on a wire ring are glued into the center. Red wool is looped around the outside edge, and cardboard is glued onto the back.

The cheerful pointed hat can be designed in many themes.

GRINCH/ELF HAT

A funny welcome not only on St. Nicholas Day! The pointed cap forms the centerpiece and is made from a cardboard triangle, with a curved tip made of wire. Ribbons, balls, bobbles and stars are wrapped or glued around it. Long hanging ribbons are a great eye-catcher. The cap is fastened to a straw wreath base wrapped with arborvitae branches that are secured with pintle wires.

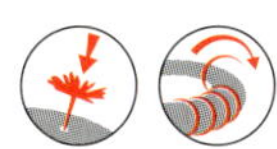

SPOTTED AND DOTTED

A straw wreath wrapped in tree-of-life branches serves as the base for this design. It is then accentuated with wide ribbons. Pin the two fabric stars with a long decorative-headed pin. Thanks to the bobble garland, the colorful balls can be spread around the wreath in no time at all.

Attention to detail: Decorative pins provide security as well as that certain something.

TEXTILE CENTER POINT

  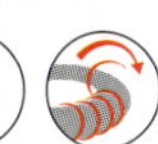

Wrap a straw wreath base with coniferous evergreens, ribbons and the like. Fasten a circle of fabric in the center, from the back, with pins. Glue long ribbons to the back of the star, and pin them, too.

HARMONIOUS LIAISON

A straw wreath covered with coniferous evergreens and a wood wreath refined with metallic leaf make a great connection. Cinnamon sticks are glued to the wood wreath.

SPRING

When nature awakens from its hibernation, tender bulb flowers such as tulips, daffodils, hyacinths and grape hyacinths will bewitch you with their charm. Bulbs alone are naturally beautiful design elements for spring-like wreaths, but eggs, in all colors and sizes, are also welcome ornaments, especially at Easter. In addition to flowers, feathers, rabbit figures, and bare and flowering branches can also be combined. Welcome the spring!

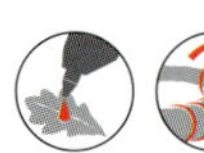

POT GARDEN

A refined contrast is created by the orange-colored binding wire, which affixes the green blueberry branches laid atop a straw wreath. Clay pots with grape hyacinths and winter aconites, as well as quail eggs, are glued on.

TEXTILE ACCENTS

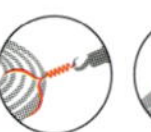
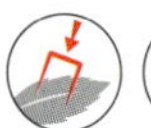

Pin hay and scraps of cloth, in bundles, to a straw wreath. Glued-on quail eggs and a wired-on water tube containing a fresh fritillary and leafy dogwood branches set accents.

BLOOMING FORKED BRANCH

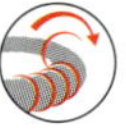

The highlight of this straw wreath wrapped in moss is an attached branch in which water tubes holding spring flowers are placed into drilled holes.

TIP

Use elongated, flexible branches for the base. Interweave these so that they form the desired wreath shape.

RADIANT DAFFODILS

Small daffodils with bulbs, white eggs, fluffy pussy willows and various strips of fabric, which are pinned, glued or knotted between the twisted willow branches, spread the spring mood in a living room.

FASHIONABLE DRESS

A particularly uncomplicated wall decoration is the straw wreath loosely wrapped with blueberry branches and colored cord. The water tube is also given a fashionable dress with yellow cord, which makes the flowers shine even brighter.

Wrap the glass tube completely with string, and tie it to the wreath.

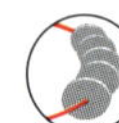

EASTER DANCE

Double round! Inside a wreath of white willow branches, adorned by fluffy catkins and feathers, fresh green eggs, threaded on string, form an Easter dance. This is simply tied to the branches. Ribbons play around the arrangement.

Whole and half quail eggs are hot-glued onto a dry-floral-foam wreath form.

SHELL CHIC

Tulips attached to their bulbs have a particularly long shelf life and are held in place in this wreath design with toothpicks. After they have faded, they can be easily exchanged. Sisal fiber is wrapped around the dry-floral-foam wreath form, and broken quail egg shells are glued on.

Fold pieces of burlap loosely, and attach them to a straw wreath base with pins.

BURLAP EGG NEST

For this casual Easter decoration, burlap is cut into pieces and folded around the straw wreath, secured with greening pins. Then hot-glue the blown and partly colored eggs into the burlap. Finally, knot blue raffia to hang the wreath with, and let it hang down.

EGGS, EGGS, EGGS

No two quail eggs are the same. If they are glued close together onto a straw wreath, an Easter mural is created. Glued-in bits of moss fill the gaps. A variety of long ribbons adds an appealing touch.

Attach pieces of bark, quail eggs, feathers and permanent flowers with hot-glue.

BIRCH BASE

Glue a narrow straw wreath atop a larger birch-bark wreath, and add materials such as artificial grape hyacinths, feathers, eggs and silver leaves.

CLEVERLY THREADED

For this colorful wall wreath, paper squares are threaded onto aluminum wire and loosely decorated with branches. A hanging pendant in the center draws attention.

The irregular shape of the wreath is created by wrapping a straw wreath thicker in some places with moss.

FEATHERED VISITORS

The highlight of this modern wall decoration are the glass birds embellished with spray paint, which have settled on branches that are also painted. A straw wreath is used as the base and is wrapped in moss, covered with pussy-willow branches and loosely tied with ribbons.

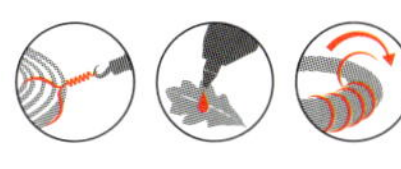

EASTER NEST

Ceramic bunnies have made themselves comfortable in this lush green boxwood wreath. They are glued to a bent wire, which is inserted into the straw wreath base. The hanging glass tubes, filled with fritillaries, are threaded into decorative wire holders, which are inserted into the straw wreath base.

By using fabric flowers, a permanent decoration for door and wall is created.

PEPPED UP

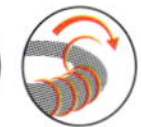

A straw wreath wrapped in boxwood can also be spiced up for spring with permanent white blossoms and bulbs.

FLORAL INTERIOR

The inside of the ready-made wreath of broom honeymyrtle is covered with permanent flowers as well as olive branches, silver leaves, sea lavender, quail eggs and feathers.

BUNNIES IN THE PIT

The loose frame made of weeping-willow branches creates the impression of a small nest for the Easter bunny and quail eggs. For the base, a straw wreath is covered with boxwood. Ribbons and accessories, like eggs, figurine and feathers, are affixed with hot glue.

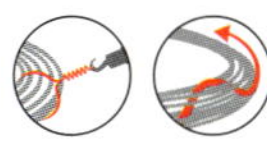

LARCH WREATH

In spring and at Eastertime, a wreath doesn't always have to be circular; an egg-shaped design can be a dramatic alternative. Various white bulb flowers are asymmetrically worked into the twisted, hand-shaped larch branches and are fastened with wire.

For a while, blooms on bulbs can do without water.

The wire loops created during the twisting technique can be cut off.

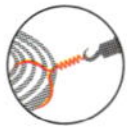

DRILLED BRANCHES

The primitive pear-tree branches are characterized by brittle rigidity, and branched pieces form this wreath, affixed using the drill technique. With permanent grape hyacinths, which are simply woven through, it becomes a permanent adornment.

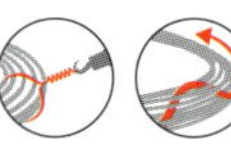

REFINED SPIRAL

Permanent hyacinths and paper cord add splashes of color to this natural wreath. Branches of weeping willow and yellow twigs are formed into rings and spirals, interwoven, and affixed with wire.

The spiral shape of the weeping-willow branches creates a dynamic effect.

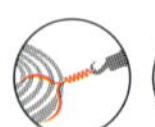

SPRING AWAKENING

Magnolia blossoms herald spring not only in the great outdoors but also as permanent flowers in a handmade wreath formed of twisted twigs of winged spindle bush.

The slender green ranunculus branches are particularly flexible.

BLUE BLOSSOMS

In this wreath of twisted ranunculus branches, which are bound here and there with paper-covered binding wire, loosely distributed permanent forget-me-nots provide spring flair. A loop made of unwound braid serves as a hanger.

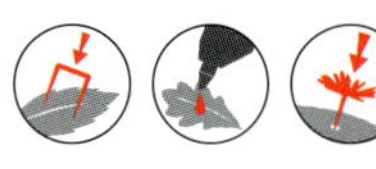

FINE ACCENTS

The simple piece of jewelry on a door shines in white, green and natural hues. Various permanent blossoms are worked into a dry-floral-foam wreath form covered with broom honeymyrtle branches, and glued-on quail eggs and feathers create subtle accents.

The bulbs are affixed onto the dry-floral-foam wreath form with toothpicks.

INTERLUDE

The spaces in this vine wreath are adorned with woven-in permanent flowers, moss and leaves, which are hot-glued in. A distinctive ribbon treatment lends elegance.

GREEN BACKDROP

Blueberry twigs inserted into a dry-floral-foam wreath form create the green background for permanent flowers, willow twigs, bulbs and dry grass, which are glued in.

Wire is wrapped around the shiny ornaments in several places and inserted into the wreath.

DECORATIVE ARCHES

White rattan reeds, which are formed into small arcs on the outside of a dry-floral-foam wreath form, stylishly frames the spring mix. The base is covered with moss, then decorated with various permanent flowers, dried fruits and decorative ornaments.

ETERNAL JOY OF BLOOMING

Spring blossom fireworks for the wall: Permanent ranunculuses, lilies, forsythia, and jasmine and cherry blossoms shine in all the colors of the rainbow. Underneath is a straw wreath, into which the flowers and vines are inserted. Small birch-bark-covered wreaths, which are decorated with colorful ribbons, are cute eye-catchers.

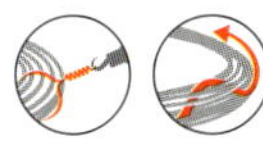

DELICATE BRANCHES OF FLOWERS

Cherry blossom branches and ranunculuses, whose flowering times overlap for only a short time in the wild, are permanently intertwined here. Shape the artificial branches into a wreath, and secure them with paper-covered binding wire. Then wire in the permanent flowers, as well.

Paper-covered binding wire ensures a firm hold on artificial branches and flowers.

 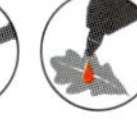 

WOODY NOTE

Here, too, faux flowers form a permanent wall decoration. For the base, glue a dry-floral-foam wreath form onto a decorative ring of wood discs, and attach narrow berry wreaths around the outside and inside perimeters with peg wire. Blossoms, bundles of grass, branches and quail eggs are affixed with hot-glue and/or wire.

SUMMER

In the sunny season, you can spend time outside again. You can discover all kinds of natural materials on a foray through the woods and pathways that can be used in creative door and wall decorations. Whether magnificent flowers in all the colors of the rainbow, wonderfully fragrant herbs, or lush green twigs and grasses, you are guaranteed to find more than you are looking for! And those who love it permanently can fall back on faux flowers or use a variety of ribbons and textiles. Your creations are guaranteed to last all summer!

A straw wreath is first wrapped with light-colored wool so that nothing shows through the attached paper.

PAPER AND BLOOM

This wall decoration exudes summery lightness through the bright colors and the openwork weaving. First, a small straw wreath base is wrapped with wool and then covered with various fine pieces of paper. Secure it to a ready-made braided wreath with pintle wires. Permanent orchids, tendrils and leaves are simply inserted into the latter.

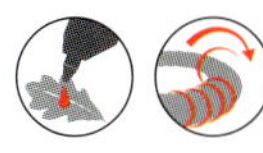

SEGMENTED JEWELRY

A simple vine or twig wreath can be converted into a flowery eye-catcher in just a few simple steps. For this, permanent flowers, such as sweet peas and hydrangeas, are attached to the lower area with hot glue. The frame is then knotted with ribbons.

COVERED ALL AROUND

Artificial flowers, ribbons and accessories can form beautiful wreaths. Here, larkspurs, hydrangeas, sedum plants, viburnum and snail shells are secured to a vine wreath form with hot glue. Then, the wreath is wrapped with ribbons and cord.

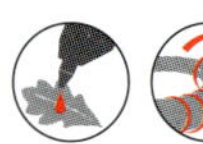

WOOD BORDER

The ready-made wreath, fashioned of rustic pieces of wood, is a naturally beautiful base for permanent flowers in cream and rose hues. Roses, chrysanthemums, ornamental onions, thistles, sweet peas, hydrangeas, rosemary and green twigs are attached with hot glue. Place dried muhlenbeckia tendrils on top, and wrap with decorative wire.

STRIPE LOOK

Permanent florals and dried fern fronds are worked into the gaps in a rattan reed ring wreath base. Hot glue is used to secure the elements.

BLUE BLOODED

Dried hydrangea blossoms, as well as permanent delphiniums, snowballs and ornamental onions, are glued in the middle of the thick wreath form, as a round dance. Color-coordinated ribbons add the finishing touches.

Permanent flowers can be easily hot-glued to fabric ribbons.

FLOWER TAIL

This white bark wreath is hung with a variety of ribbons in pastel colors. This creates an attractive tail onto which roses, delphiniums, grasses, hydrangeas, dogwood, muhlenbeckia tendrils, wild garlic and dried fern fronds are attached with hot-glue.

Three wreaths, three techniques. With the artichoke wreath, the leaves are attached to the surface in an overlapping manner with hot-glue.

WREATH CHAIN

These various wreaths are made from artichoke or olive leaves, which are attached to dry-floral-foam wreath forms with pins or glued on in a scale-like manner. It gets wilder with a wrap of lavender, thyme and globe thistles. Tie the wreaths to each other according to their size with coconut coir fiber rope, and hang them up.

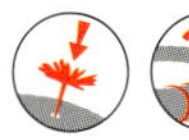

AROMA OF THE SOUTH

A pleasant scent is spread by bundled lavender and thyme on the wreath form, which is wrapped in milkweed and then decorated. There are also olive branches and globe thistles, and garlic adds visual and aromatic accents. Finally, attach the wreath onto a wood tray.

FRAMED WREATH

Mediterranean elements such as olive branches, lavender, rosemary, thyme and sage come together to form a wild swirl of herbs. A wire wreath ring serves as a base. When glued to a framed board, the wreath becomes a particularly beautiful wall decoration.

HERBAL LUST

Between green leaves, this wreath shines with burgundy red, purple and blue hues. Lavender, ornamental onions, rosemary, basil, dill, sage and star-flower bush are wrapped around a straw wreath base, and dry grass surrounds the whole design. With permanent herbs, it stays radiantly beautiful while fresh botanicals dry decoratively.

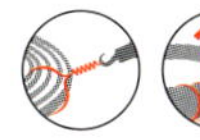

LINED UP

In rank and file, lavender, rosemary, sage, thyme, curry bush, laurel and feverfew are each grouped into small bundles. Wrap a wire wreath ring with hay for the base. Around this, tie the fragrant bundles tightly on both sides.

Paper-covered binding wire holds the bundles of herbs together and is a decorative eye-catcher.

GREEN SEASONING

For this wreath of herbs all in green, a straw wreath base is wrapped lushly with sage, rosemary and the like. Without flowers, it will last a relatively long time, even with fresh herbs.

FRAGRANCE BUNDLE

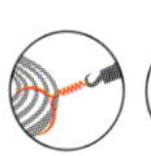

Individual bundles of lavender and oats are wired onto a straw wreath base, which is wrapped in herbs and flowers.

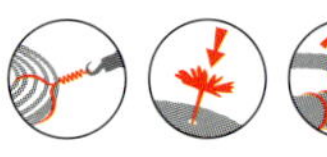

FLOWER TUBES

The middle of a straw mat, wrapped with moss and then covered with blueberry branches, is filled with birch-bark tubes and water tubes covered with paper, which are held in place with paper-covered binding wire. Add flowers to the filled water tubes. A variety of crisscrossing ribbons round off the design.

RIBBONS OF ALL KINDS

Here, blueberry branches are accentuated with natural, light-green and white ribbons, and wool. Pinch in some pieces of coordinating decorative paper at the bottom.

CASUAL STRAWS

With this coiled piece of jewelry, a few stalks can stick out cheekily. Grass knots hang on colorful braids. A straw wreath is suitable as a base.

Place the thick side of the wire mesh against the thin side of the boxwood wreath and vice versa.

HEADSTAND

Two interlocking wreaths form the frame for the immortelle flowers, which are hung upside down with a cord of the same color. For the wreath form, boxwood is wrapped around a wire wreath ring and thickened on one side. The counterpart can easily be formed from wadded windling wire.

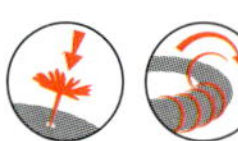

COUNTRY FLAIR

Red-and-white wall decorations for the country house kitchen: A straw wreath, which is first wrapped with ribbons and then with tea towels, is given the finishing touch by a water tube filled with fresh summer flowers. The water tube is banded with red cord and attached with a wood pick. Pins and wood picks also help secure the cloths in place.

For the garland, create flags of masking tape with different patterns along the red cord.

A DIFFERENT WAY OF CULINARY HERBS

The narrow rosemary wreath is simple but effective. The branches are easily wrapped around a wire wreath ring. Red-and-white checked ribbon adds a rural touch.

SHOW THE FLAG

A ready-made whitewashed branch wreath form can be spiced up in a flash with glued-on red artificial berries and a homemade garland made of cord and masking-tape flags.

FLOWER POWER

As a party decoration or a nice accessory for a home: This wreath comprises a smaller straw wreath base wrapped in wool that is wired inside a larger wet-floral-foam wreath form. Cover the floral-foam wreath with flowers, and then attach thyme and burdock with liquid floral adhesive/cold glue.

PEARL LUSTER

Pearls, wool, ribbons and grass combine to create a green decorative object for a wall or door. Wrap a straw wreath with stems of grass, wrapping the grass with wire to hold it in place. Grass and wool are either coiled into snails and fixed with decorative pins or braided and knotted around the wreath in the lower area. Pearls threaded onto wire and long decorative ribbons add further accents.

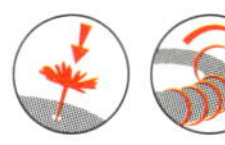

THE MOUNTAIN CALLS

This alpine specimen earns admiring glances not only in front of an impressive mountain panorama but also at home. Felt and wool, in green, orange and gray, are particularly eye-catching and are wrapped around the grass-covered straw wreath base or coiled into snails and pinned on. Allow the grass to show through in some places.

For the snails made of grass or wool, the strips are wrapped with wire and then coiled.

BRAIDING

Broad wool threads in varying hues of green are woven into a long braid, which is wrapped around the wreath and pinned in place. Accentuate with jewel-headed pins.

PIMPED UP GRASSES

At top and bottom of this wreath, wide gray strips of felt, each equipped with a coiled grass snail, adorn a green-grass-covered straw wreath. Ribbons add color.

TECHNIQUES

There are various aids and techniques for designing and embellishing door and wall wreaths; these are presented and explained in detail on the following pages. Whether a straw wreath, wire ring or floral-foam base, the selection of the right underlay is crucial. Subsequently, the techniques of threading, twisting and wiring, sticking, gluing, plugging, and winding are taught in images and text. You can determine which of these techniques were used to create the wreaths in this book by the corresponding icons.

WREATH FORMS

For almost all wreaths, with the exception of twisted specimens, you need a base, which you can then embellish as you wish. Whether it is a straw wreath, a floral-foam wreath form, a Styrofoam wreath form, a vine wreath or a wire ring, the selection is important and, in some cases, dictates the techniques or materials to be used. In this way, all wreaths can be wrapped around, but not all of them can be cut out, pinned into or glue onto. So, the choice also depends on the materials you want to use.

STRAW WREATH

It is probably the most common wreath base, and it can be wrapped, glued onto or cut out. In preparation, it should be prepared with Roman wrapping tape (wreath gusset tape), which is available crepe or fleece; it makes the surface more pleasant to work on. It is also green in color and prevents the straw from showing through.

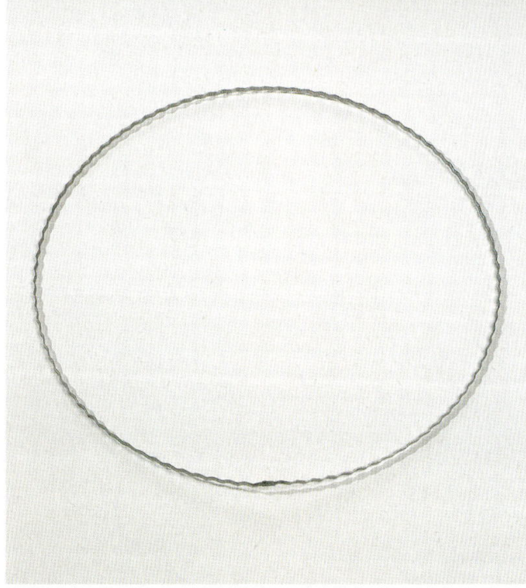

WIRE RING

It is particularly suitable for very narrow, filigree wreaths. Wire rings are made from round or flat and smooth or corrugated wire. The slightly corrugated form is easier to grip and helps prevent wound materials from slipping. These hold even better if the ring is first covered all around with stem wrap tape.

FLORAL-FOAM WREATH FORM

For hanging wreaths, dry-floral-foam wreath forms are best suited for dried and permanent botanicals. If you choose a wet-floral-foam wreath form, in order to be able to design with fresh flowers, you should wrap it with cling film to prevent drips.

TIP

Many wreath forms (for example, those made with coniferous evergreens), can be bought ready-made.

THREADING

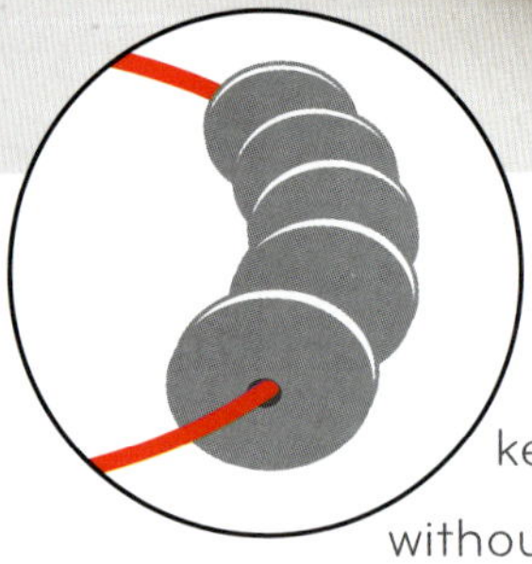

By threading leaves, fruits, flowers and the like, you can create narrow wreaths. All florals must be able to be kept for a long enough time for this type of processing without a water supply. Materials are usually impaled on a wire and lined up close together. No further tools are required for soft materials, whereas harder materials such as chestnuts, eggs or nuts have to be drilled. In addition to wire, thread, string or cord can be used for threading.

HOW-TO

THREADING

Harder materials, such as chestnuts, must first be drilled.

Then, they can simply be threaded onto wire.

CHAINS

Alternatively, materials can also be wired to form a ring.

Always keep the same distance, and bring the ends together.

TIP

To work in the gaps in fruit, guide the wire back and pierce it a second time. Tighten the resulting loop to prevent it from slipping.

DRILL & CONNECT

Wires can be used in many ways when designing wreaths. They serve as insertion aids for cones and the like, they can bind and hold materials such as moss or tendrils on a wreath base, or they can even form the basic shapes themselves, such as rings or braids. As a rule, they are made of iron, are lightly oiled to prevent rust and must be stored in a dry place. Depending on the technology, a distinction is made, for example, between pintle wire, winding wire or twist wire. The latter has eyelets and is used for the fixing drill technique.

LIGAMENT TAILS

Long flowing ribbon tails or ribbon-loop cascades are beautiful decorative elements for wall and door wreaths. To create these, bring the lengths together in the middle at one point, and secure with wire that is tightly wrapped around several times. Important: There must be two long wire ends left with which the ribbons can then be inserted into the wreath base.

CHRISTMAS BALLS

Ornaments are often used in Christmas wreaths. The wire is attached in the area of the transition from the actual ball to the ball neck, which is covered by the suspension crown. To do this, carefully wrap the ball neck with thin-gauge wire once or twice. Because the wire can slip off easily, adding a drop of hot glue will help.

DRILLING TECHNIQUE

The twisting of rebar tie wires, each with an eyelet at both ends, saves time and effort with a twister. The wire is wrapped around the materials, and both wire eyelets are hooked into the device hook. Then, pull the handle of the device, and hold the connection point firmly. The inner part of the twister with the hook rotates around its own axis and twirls the wire ends.

HOW-TO

WIRE ON THE PIN

Pull the wire tightly between the lower rows of cone scales.

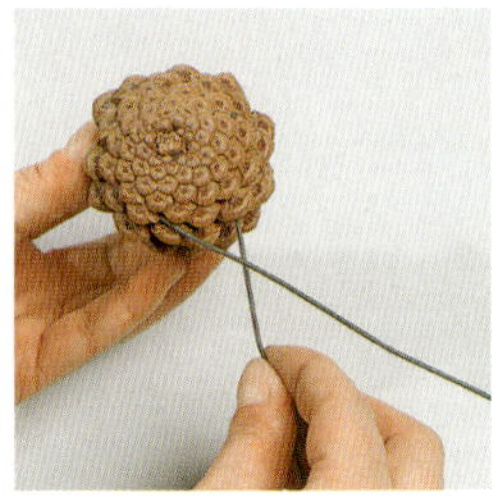

The wire ends must cross where they emerge from the cone.

Twist at least two or three times.

Wrong: If you leave the wire untwisted, it will come loose from the scales.

WIRE LOOPS

Gather the bow loops in the middle, and place a hairpin wire over it.

Loop the end of the ribbon over the wire and between the wire hairpin.

Secure the knot loops by twisting the wire ends.

Knot the narrower second ribbon on the back of the bow.

TIP

Rebar tie wire twisting tool

WIRE PINS

With the adhesive techniques, flat materials can be attached to various substrates. For example, leaves and small pieces of moss or paper can be used that would be difficult to process with the winding technique and would be cut by a lashed wire. Pins (or clips) are available in different sizes and shapes. Roman stirrups have a straight bracket; greening pins or patent sticks have a wavy bracket; and hairpins (or staples) have a semicircular bracket.

HOW-TO

ATTACH MOSS

In the case of flat rag moss, the wrapping of a straw wreath base can be omitted.

Long-legged wire hair-pins are used for thick flat moss.

ATTACH LEAVES

Insert the wire pins as far down as possible on the base of the leaf.

Some leaves can also be rolled and then pinned into or adhered to the wreath base.

ATTACH TWIGS AND TENDRILS

Coniferous evergreen branches can also be fixed by pinning them onto the wreath base.

Tendrils and other similar materials are usually attached in the same manner.

ATTACH TO FRESH FLORAL FOAM

In the case of a layer with rigid foam, you can pin to the side of the wreath base.

Moss can also be attached to floral foam with hairpin-shaped wires or greening pins.

TIP

In the case of clips, the width of the upper bracket and the length of the two legs are given in millimeters.

GLUE

Anything that cannot inserted into or wired onto a wreath base easily can be glued on. The hot-glue gun is often the first choice as an aid here, but is suitable only for dry things. In addition, mostly hard accessories, such as nuts and eggs, or, less often, soft accessories such as fabrics and fibers, can be secured with hot-glue. Hot-glue must never be used for fresh materials such as flowers and leaves because the glue would burn them. Liquid floral adhesive (a.k.a. floral glue or cold glue) is suitable for such purposes.

HOW-TO

HOT-GLUE

Make sure that the adhesive surfaces are small but still sufficiently large for the hold.

Caution: Do not apply too much glue, and avoid glue threads.

LIQUID FLORAL ADHESIVE, FLORAL GLUE, COLD GLUE

Hairy and hairless leaves can be glued on their undersides.

Even flower petals can be adhered in no time with liquid floral adhesive.

TIP

Hot-glue guns are used to melt and apply hot glue. Pay attention to the dangers of electrical current and the risk of burns. Guns that are in use must not be laid down; instead, they must be placed upright because, otherwise, the adhesive can flow back into the gun and stick the mechanism.

PICKS

Depending on the material and substrate, this technique may not necessarily require an aid. Real or permanent flower stems, twigs and tendrils can be inserted directly into dry or wet flower foam, wire mesh or vine wreaths. If a straw wreath is used as a base, additional aids such as toothpicks, pins, wood picks or pintle wire are required. This means, for example, that wreaths can be decorated with bulbs, fruits, cones, paper, fabric and ribbons.

PINS

A straw wreath is particularly suitable as a base for affixing materials with pins. For example, the ends of ribbons as well as fabrics, pieces of paper or leaves can be fastened almost invisibly. Even small applications can be attached quickly. If you want to affix additional accents, use pins with decorative heads.

TOOTHPICKS

Toothpicks are another popular tool for inserting materials into straw and dry- and wet-floral-foam wreath forms. They can be used to skewer fruits and vegetables, such as ornamental apples, ornamental quinces, berries or bulbs, and attach them to a wreath base. This is particularly quick, and the toothpicks remain invisible.

TIP

The selection of the wreath and, if necessary, the aids for pinning depends on the floral and materials used.

PINTLE WIRE

Harder materials and decorative objects, such as cones, cannot be attached with pins or toothpicks. They must be wired, and then the wire ends inserted into the wreath base. For this, we recommend pintle wire, which, unlike support wire, is sharpened on one end. This means that twigs, flowers and leaves can also be attached to a harder base, such as a straw wreath.

WITHOUT AIDS

Dry-or wet-floral-foam wreath forms usually require no aids to incorporate flowers because flower and leaf stems, as well as twigs—real or permanent—can be inserted directly into the substrate. In the case of thicker stems, cut them at an angle before inserting them. This makes them more pointed and easier to insert.

WRAPS

Not all wraps are the same: this technique offers varying possibilities. On one hand, by wrapping wire, cord and the like, applied natural materials, such as moss or twigs, can be fixed on a wreath base—almost invisibly or as a visible accent. On the other hand, the base can also be sheathed with ribbons, wool or fabrics. In these cases, the wrapping material is usually not an aid for attaching materials but serves as a decorative element itself.

WINDING WIRE (A.K.A. PADDLE OR SPOOL WIRE)

Winding wire refers to wire rolled on spools or wood paddles, for binding various materials onto a base such as a dry-floral-foam wreath form, a straw wreath or a willow hoop. Winding wire is available in different thicknesses (gauges) and colors, but is usually hardly noticeable.

SET COLORED ACCENTS

Compared to winding wire, paper-covered binding wire, cord or wool deliberately attract attention. They serve to afffix natural materials on a wreath base, but they also act as a design element. They are available in many colors, so they can be used to set great accents.

TIP

Coniferous evergreen branches are especially good for winding up on a wreath base.

HOW-TO

TIE THE WREATH BODY

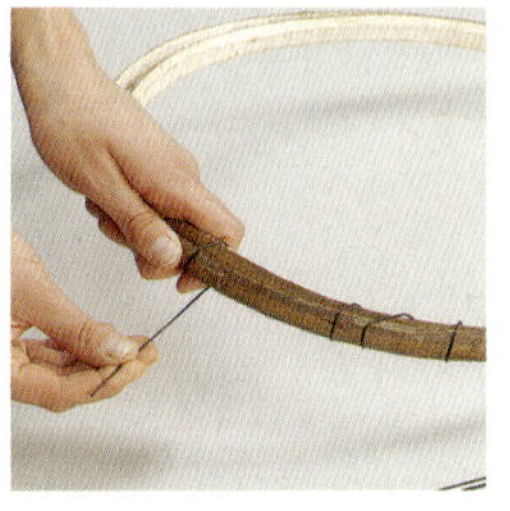

Bend willow reeds to the desired size, and secure with wire.

Attach branches of foliage to the reed wreath form as a base to be wrapped around.

Wire coniferous evergreen branches into a wreath form.

Alternatively, moss can be used.

WRAP A STRAW WREATH

Wrap a straw wreath with green crepe or fleece Roman wrapping tape (wreath gusset tape).

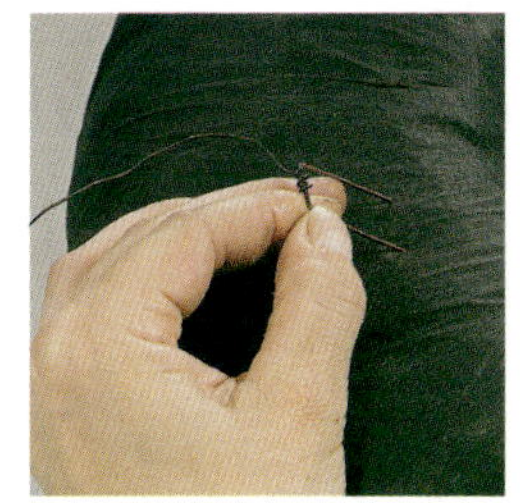

The winding wire is attached to the wreath with a hairpin-shaped wire or greening pin.

Place materials atop the wrapped wreath, and secure them by wrapping with spool or paddle wire.

Create a loop, guide the end of the wire around the wreath, and twist.

FIXED IN SHAPE

Pliable branches, such olive branches, can be easily bundled and wrapped with paper-covered binding wire or cord. Then join the bundles together to form a wreath. The binding wire remains visible in these cases.

WINDING

Winding is the only wreath technique that does not require a base. However, a wire ring can be used for additional strength and shape. Long flexible twigs and tendrils are usually used for the basic structure. These are interwoven in such a way that they form the desired wreath shape. If necessary, decorative wire, paper-covered binding wire, raffia or cord can be used to bind the materials together fixation, and they are simply twisted or knotted around the branches.

TIP

For branches with thorns, wear gloves for protection.

HOW-TO

Dense or loose wreaths are created from tendrils, vines and flexible twigs.

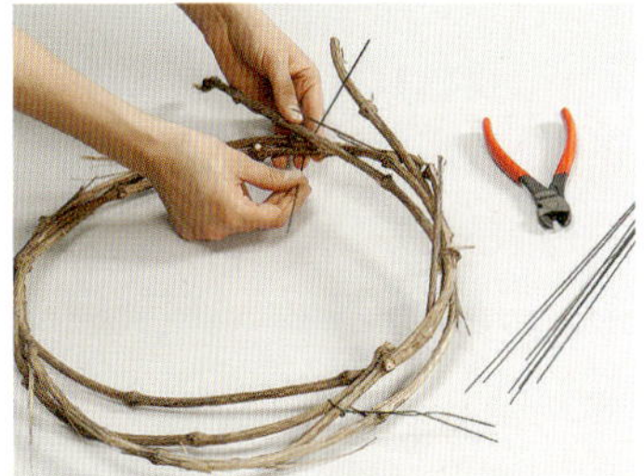

Thicker tendrils should be bound with wire ensure stability.

Twist and interweave the tendrils to create a wreath form.

If necessary, secure with raffia, decorative wire or binding wire.

OTHER BOOKS PUBLISHED BY WILDFLOWER MEDIA

CREATIVITY: A GLOBAL FLORAL INTROSPECTIVE
PRICE: $24.95 / **ISBN:** 978-1-7337826-5-4

FLOWERS TO WEAR: THE FASCINATION OF FLORAL COUTURE
PRICE: $27.95 / **ISBN:** 978-1-7337826-7-8

ITALIAN WEDDING BOUQUETS
PRICE: $19.99 / **ISBN:** 978-1-7355603-0-4

ITALIAN FLORAL ARTISTRY
PRICE: $19.99 / **ISBN:** 978-1-7337826-0-9

FALLING INTO FLOWERS: A STEP-BY-STEP GUIDE TO TODAY'S MODERN WEDDING BUSINESS
PRICE: $19.99 / **ISBN:** 978-1-7337826-9-2

FLOWER ARRANGING: A STEP-BY-STEP GUIDE TO FLORAL DESIGN
PRICE: $39.95 / **ISBN:** 978-1-7337826-2-3

KOREAN COCOJI: TRADITIONAL KOREAN FLOWER ARRANGEMENT
PRICE: $14.99 / **ISBN:** 978-1-7337826-4-7

IMPERMANENT
PRICE: $29.95 / **ISBN:** 978-1-7337826-8-5

SEASONS: A CURATED SELECTION OF TIMELY TECHNIQUES FROM THE PAGES OF FLORISTS' REVIEW MAGAZINE
PRICE: $24.95 / **ISBN:** 978-1-7337826-1-6

SLOW FLOWERS JOURNAL
PRICE: $24.95 / **ISBN:** 978-1-7337826-3-0

IN LOVE: INSPIRATIONAL EUROPEAN WEDDING BOUQUETS
PRICE: $24.95 / **ISBN:** 978-1-7355603-2-8

READY, SET, DESIGN!: YOUR GUIDE TO BECOMING AN AWARD-WINNING FLORAL DESIGNER
PRICE: $24.95 / **ISBN:** 978-1-7355603-4-2

WE LOVE DRIED FLOWERS: HANDMADE WREATHS, ROOM DECORATIONS & BOUQUETS
PRICE: $24.95 / **ISBN:** 978-1-7355603-5-9

ARTISTIC FLORAL ARTISTRY: INNOVATIVE WORK FROM THE AMERICAN INSTITUTE OF FLORAL DESIGNERS
PRICE: $34.99 / **ISBN:** 978-1-7337826-6-1

CREATIVE FLOWER ARRANGING: A STEP-BY-STEP GUIDE
PRICE: $26.95 / **ISBN:** 978-0-9935715-3-4

SHOP ALL OF OUR NEW TITLES TO INSPIRE, EDUCATE AND GROW YOUR FLORAL BUSINESS!

VISIT US ONLINE AT SHOP.WILDFLOWER.MEDIA

CREDITS

EDITOR BLOOM's GmbH, Ratingen, www.blooms.de
STYLING Klaus Wagener, Team BLOOM's
REDACTION Hella Henckel, Laura Marx
IDEA, CONCEPTION AND TEXT Laura Marx
WREATH DESIGNS All ideas from Team BLOOM's, except: Page 016 above: Ingrid Menzi-Sprenger; Page 016 below: Petra Schwarz; Page 017: Sylvia Mock; Page 018 left: Susanne Roppel; Page 018 right: Monika Grosberger; Page 019: Sonja Kraus; Page 023: Eva-Maria Heublein - all participants of BLOOM's autumn Workshops in Leitlhof, Innichen/I in October 2016; Page 045 below right: Florist Marion Schmid, Blumen Elsberger-Weiss, Kolbermoor; Page 054 below: Flowers Engler, Leipzig, from the Advent Exhibition 2008; Pages 098 and 099: Participants in the BLOOM's summer workshop at DAS KRONTHALER June 2015.
PHOTOS Patrick Pantze Images GmbH, Lage
More photos: Yang Junjie, Unsplash.com (Page 004); Brooke Lark, Unsplash.com (Pages 084–085)
GRAHIC DESIGN Adriani Schmidt DTP; Britta Baschen, DRUCK company group APPL, aprinta druck GmbH, Wemding, Germany

U.S. Edition 2021
ISBN 978-1-7355603-6-6

Published in the United States
by WildFlower Media Inc.
© BLOOM's GmbH
https://Shop.WildFlower.Media

Wildflower.Media

Info@WildFlower.Media

THE AUTHOR

As the managing editor of the lifestyle magazine BLOOM's DECO, Laura Marx deals daily with current trends and products that make homes more beautiful. Together with the BLOOM's team, she constantly presents new decorations, gift and DIY ideas on the subjects of flowers and plants that encourage imitation.